अनवॉइसेड हार्ट

ज्योति वर्मा

Copyright © Jyoti Verma
All Rights Reserved.

This book has been self-published with all reasonable efforts taken to make the material error-free by the author. No part of this book shall be used, reproduced in any manner whatsoever without written permission from the author, except in the case of brief quotations embodied in critical articles and reviews.

The Author of this book is solely responsible and liable for its content including but not limited to the views, representations, descriptions, statements, information, opinions and references ["Content"]. The Content of this book shall not constitute or be construed or deemed to reflect the opinion or expression of the Publisher or Editor. Neither the Publisher nor Editor endorse or approve the Content of this book or guarantee the reliability, accuracy or completeness of the Content published herein and do not make any representations or warranties of any kind, express or implied, including but not limited to the implied warranties of merchantability, fitness for a particular purpose. The Publisher and Editor shall not be liable whatsoever for any errors, omissions, whether such errors or omissions result from negligence, accident, or any other cause or claims for loss or damages of any kind, including without limitation, indirect or consequential loss or damage arising out of use, inability to use, or about the reliability, accuracy or sufficiency of the information contained in this book.

Made with ♥ on the Notion Press Platform
www.notionpress.com

क्रम-सूची

Words Of Soul Publication ... vii

प्रस्तावना ... ix

1. Jyoti Verma ... 1

अधूरी मोहब्बत

2. Raunak Kumar Saha ... 5

SABAK

3. Kalpesh Pramod Bharambe ... 9

4. जिंदगी ... 10

5. Sabrin Sultan ... 11

HE WILL HEAL YOU

6. Samridhi Fagnia ... 15

DEPRESSION IS PAIN. THE WORST KIND OF SUFFERING

7. Har Deepansh Bahadur Sinha ... 21

प्यार एक जंग

8. Noor Tabassum ... 25

CRY OF THE BROKEN HEART

9. Emerald Reshma Reddithota ... 29

UNVOICED HEART

10. Shubhanjali Nishad ... 33

टाईटल- एक नया दर्द

11. Anveshitha ... 37

NOTHING LEFT

12. Neelaksh ... 41

WHY YOU BROKE MY HEART

13. Manik Gupta ... 45

WITHOUT YOU

क्रम-सूची

14. Ranbir Bhakat 49

INNER ME

15. Shireesha M V 53

EMPOWERING IGNORANCE

16. Bishakha Kumari Saxena 57

पहली बार जब दिल टूटा

17. Raghavi Raghu 63

TIME

18. Salma Khan 67

MERI TRUE LOVE STORY

19. Aabid Subzar 71

THE UNVOICED

20. Kamini Pradhan 75

कहते कुछ नहीं

21. Nayan Datey 79

Andaaz E ISHQ

22. Sanat Kumar Mishra 83

HIS HEART CRIPPLED

23. Swathi R 87

MY EYES AREN'T GONNA SHINE ANYMORE

24. Amrutha C 91

OH,HEART,YOU WERE THE ONE

25. Ritu 95

SAMJHA LIJIYE

26. Ishita 99

A BETTER PLACE

क्रम-सूची

27. Sapana S Bain   103

LONE TEARS

• v •

Words Of Soul Publication

वड्र्स ऑफ सोल एक राइटिंग कम्युनिटी है, जहां हमारे पास नए नवोदित लेखकों का एक समूह है, जो भावनाओं को शब्दों में ढालने की अपनी प्रतिभा के साथ हैं।

उत्साही लेखकों को प्रोत्साहित करने और उनकी सराहना करने के लिए 15 मई 2021 को डॉ. निकिता दुदागी और लकी पांडे द्वारा गठित समुदाय के सर्वश्रेष्ठ लेखक को पहचानने के लिए साप्ताहिक विशेष कार्यक्रम और कार्यक्रम आयोजित किए जा रहे हैं। वड्र्स ऑफ सोल, महत्वाकांक्षी लेखकों का एक समूह जो पाठक के मन को प्रेरित करने के लिए अपने दिल की भावनाओं को स्याही करता है।

वड्र्स ऑफ सोल पब्लिकेशन केवल एक प्रकाशन नहीं है, यह लेखकों का एक प्रकार का परिवार है जिसमें सह-लेखक, लेखक, लेखक, संकलक, सह-संकलक, ग्राफिक टीम, परियोजना प्रमुख, सीईओ, सह-संस्थापक और संस्थापक शामिल हैं। यहां हर कोई अपने विचार देने के लिए स्वतंत्र है

WORDS OF SOUL PUBLICATION

और हम उनके कार्यों की पहल करते हैं....

प्रस्तावना

वइर्स ऑफ़ सोल से प्रकाशित हुए संकलन "जिसका नाम अनवॉइस्ड हार्ट " है जिसमे हर जगह हैं लेखकों ने रुचि दिखाई है इसमें कुल 30 लेखकों ने अपने दिल के दबी हुआ आवाज लिखी है जो की काफ़ी दिल को छूने वाली है । इसमें कावती ,शायरी, नॉवेल अनके प्रकार के है इसमें ।

1. JYOTI VERMA

COMPILER

She is Jyoti Verma who belongs from BALLIA (UTTAR PRADESH). She is doing her ug courses from ALLAHABAD UNIVERSITY . She is writer since 10 months and work In many anthology as a co author and compiled few books yet . She had written a book named hushed voice for this she has been awarded a national award. She is interested in music and dancing also .she is a graphic designer and working in many publications as a designer.

अधूरी मोहब्बत

हमने तो समझा अपना ही उसको,
बेवफ़ा मुझे आजमाती रही उम्र भर।

सोचने तक अब नम हो जाती आँखें,
इस हद तक हमें जगाती रही उम्र भर,

कितनी हसीन शामे तेरे संग गुज़री,
वही मुलाकाते रुलाती रही उम्र भर,

कैसे इतना हद तक टूट गया था मैं,
ज़िंदगी यहीं समझाती रही उम्र भर,

तेरे बाद भी तुझसे रूठें हम कई बार,
तेरी यादे मगर मनाती रही उम्र भर,

अधूरी मोहब्बत सताती रही उम्र भर,
एक मलाल मुझे खाती रही उम्र भर ।।

2. RAUNAK KUMAR SAHA

Raunak Kumar Saha was born and brought up in West Bengal, India. He is always an ardent reader of books, and passionate to write poetry and quotes.Apart from that, he loves to listen songs and play football during his leisure time. He is currently one of the CAT aspirant , and wants to hold the position of Manager In Finance, in one of the reputed MNC.

SABAK

Jaanta nahi tha yeh mohobbat kaise kaise din dikhaegi,

Jiski sabse jyada zaroorat thi woh beech rah par akela

chod chali jaegi,

Mere rone par woh hasegi muskurayegi,

Sath hokar bhi gharwaalon ke saamne khudko akela
dikhaegi,

Mere dosto ko mere khilaaf bhadkaegi,

Mere dushmano se haath milakar woh dosti nibhaegi,

Door nahi who din jab who tadpegi pachtaegi,

Jaanta nahi tha ye mohobbat mujhe aise sabak sikhaegi ...

3. KALPESH PRAMOD BHARAMBE

Kalpesh Pramod Bharambe.He is a Hindi and Marathi Writter, Engineer,YouTuber.Writter life's Extremely Dedicated to his Country,They Covered Many Social Issues in his poetry.The writter strives to promote humanity and Inspiration through his poet's..

4. जिंदगी

अपना हो या पराया
दर्द तो हर किसी ने दिया
हर मुकाम पर नयै लोगो का सताना
रेगीस्थान के बीच खडा हुं मै अकेला
बाज तेरी उडान मुझे बक्श दे
पथरीली मिट्टी पर कोई पेर खिच रहा
आँखे तरस गयी मंजील को देखते देखते
कमजोर शरीर घावो से घायल हो गया
तनहाई पसंद लगने लगी
जहा मेरी परछाई नै दिया मुझै सहारा
अंधेरी रातो की काली परिस्थिती
जहा तुनै भी मेरा साथ छोड़ दिया
जुबान मेरी खामोश हो गयी
किसी सै रहा ना कोई रिश्ता
मेरी मंजिल मुझै मिल कर रहेगी
कलम स्याही को मान लिया मैंने अपना ।।

5. SABRIN SULTAN

Assalamualaikum Everyone! The name of this co author is Sabrin Sultan. She is a girl who prefers reading The Quran as her favourite book above anything else. She loves writing and in school, her notebooks were always full of scribbles. She has her love for writing from her fellows who always encouraged her to keep penning down her thoughts. She believes that Writing is her way of coping with all of her emotions and a way to reach out to people when other words fall short.

HE WILL HEAL YOU

To all those Broken Hearts, I would only say one thing, stay strong because you are strong. Life itself is a test, the toughest test and if you fail to survive, then you've failed the test. And why shall I be upset when my Lord in the Holy Book has already said that He is with those whose hearts are broken?

I will be patient because I know that the Lord whom I love the most will not waste the reward of the good doers. The heartbreaks that happen are a blessing because He encourages us to return to Him and that is the reason why sometimes I feel that problems are a must. If we only get pleasure and peace, then how will we remember Him? Shall we all not think before we speak because speaking out can break a heart that Allaah loves..

The healer of the hearts is The Lord who created you and me and the entire Universe. I will always remind myself that I'm not broken, I'm just being called to Him and for me to be called to Him, I'm ready to face such Heartbreaks!

6. SAMRIDHI FAGNIA

Hello

I am blogger since last 2 years on wordpress as well co-author I like to share my experiences through my blogs and want people to read more and implement more in their life !!

DEPRESSION IS PAIN. THE WORST KIND OF SUFFERING

It becomes increasingly hard to sleep at night – every morning begins on a morose note. The scariest part about depression is not the endless blanket of darkness that covers you.

The scariest thing about depression is the moment of realization that repeatedly shows that you have lost yourself.You can't sleep. You can't escape. The thoughts keep haunting you. You hear the birds chirping, the alarm clock ringing, water running down the buckets. Sunlight peeps into your room through a little crack in the window and you know it's time. Time to wake up,You feel the heat, but you don't feel warm. You feel cold, but you don't feel the calm. The wind blows in your face, but it refuses to dry the sweat inside you. It rains day and night, but your insides remain covered in dust. The sun shines everyday, but you freeze away piece by piece inside.

You feel suffocated even when the air around you is composed of oxygen. You feel trapped even when all the doors and windows in your house are wide open.You feel lonely even when you are not alone and you want to be with someone when you are alone.

You don't have the courage to move forward.

You feel so frustrated and alienated from one another.

Depression is pain. The worst kind of suffering

It becomes increasingly hard to sleep at night – every morning begins on a morose note. The scariest part about depression is not the endless blanket of darkness that covers you.

The scariest thing about depression is the moment of realization that repeatedly shows that you have lost yourself.You can't sleep. You can't escape. The thoughts keep haunting you. You hear the birds chirping, the alarm clock ringing, water running down the buckets. Sunlight peeps into your room through a little crack in the window and you know it's time. Time to wake up,You feel the heat, but you don't feel warm. You feel cold, but you don't feel the calm. The wind blows in your face, but it refuses to dry the sweat inside you. It rains day and night, but your insides remain covered in dust. The sun shines everyday, but you freeze away piece by piece inside.

You feel suffocated even when the air around you is composed of oxygen. You feel trapped even when all the doors and windows in your house are wide open.You feel lonely even when you are not alone and you want to be with someone when you are alone.

You don't have the courage to move forward.

You feel so frustrated and alienated from one another.

You don't feel happy anymore for things which made you happy earlier.

You start searching for the meaning of your life and you conclude that there is no meaning at all.

You start being sleepless and also depression makes you scared of nights.

You start pretending yourself that you were happy instead of you are.

You fail at faking a smile, you fail at pretending you are a normal person.

You cry out hell and when you are done, you overthink and cry on the same.

You feel hopeless and there is no one to help you out from this.Depression is more than being sad and it is a strength in you because there's nothing harder than overcoming demons within yourself. It is a tough time that anyone has to go through. Your life is a world of both good and bad.

Take a moment to slow down and absorb all of it.

Life is not about sitting in a corner and waiting for the storm to pass. Life is about how you learn to dance under the very storm.

It's not easy but daily efforts add up to better results

remember that the process of healing isn't a straight path.

7. HAR DEEPANSH BAHADUR SINHA

हर दीपाँश बहादुर सिन्हा लखनऊ, उत्तर प्रदेश से संबंध रखते है। इन्होंने नैशनल पोस्ट ग्रेजुएट कॉलेज से भूगोल में स्नाकोत्तर की शिक्षा ग्रहण की है। गाने सुनना, पकवान बनाना , गाड़ी चलाना इनकी रुचियाँ है। लिखना , तस्वीरे लेना , सौरमंडल को समझना और घूमने के प्रति इनका गहरा लगाव है।

प्यार एक जंग

नहीं जानता था उसके भीतर की बात

उसके बारे में सोचता रेहता दिन रात ,

हरगिज़ नहीं था मुझे इस अनहोनी का आभास

वर्ना तुम्हारे करीब आने के ना करते प्रयास ।

एक तरफ़ में था उसकी मंशा से अनजान

खुद भी चली गई और लूट ली मेरी मुस्कान ,

जब तुम्हारे दिल में थी इतनी गर्द

तो फिर मुझे क्यों दिए सारे दर्द ।

फिरता हूँ में अब बन के बंजारा

नहीं चाहिए मुझे कोई सहारा ,

चंद लम्हों को बख़ूबी सवारा

चाहता तो हूँ पर अब ना आना दोबारा ।

जिंदगी में मिली जो मुझे ठोकर

बहुत सीख मैंने खुद से बिछड़कर ,

आज भी कभी कभी आजाती तुम्हारी याद

जब एक पल में कर दिया था मुझे बर्बाद ।

आशिक़ था पर नहीं था आवारा

मिलेगा मुझे कोई तुमसे बेहद प्यारा ,

आशा करता हूँ उसे पता होगी प्रेम की परिभाषा

उम्मीद करता हूँ अब फिर से हाथ ना लगे निराशा ।।

8. NOOR TABASSUM

The name of the author is Noor Tabassum. Writing is her passion. She has participated in more than 300 anthologies as co author and has also written solo books called Sensibles and Twisted Firsts. She is a nature lover and loves to lead a simple life. She expresses all her feelings in her writings as she thinks it is the most powerful medium to communicate. She has won many writing competitions, and her articles have been published in many magazines too. She enjoys writing poems and short stories. Her stories have been published in the Times of India newspaper too.
Her Instagram id is @noortabassumali123

CRY OF THE BROKEN HEART

CRY OF THE BROKEN HEART

I pray to Almighty that you too should fall in love one day,

And let someone discrete you from your love that day,

Let this smile on your lips be wiped away,

Let your eyes also be sunk in tears every day,

Let your heart scream vociferously in this never-ending pain,

I wish you too would plead everyone, every second to confront your love,

But I wish you never get a chance to have a glance of your beloved,

Let your dreams be scattered ubiquitously,

And I wish you too try to gather them running frantically,

I wish you too undoubtedly believe in love, as I do,

Let your heart and mind always speak of your separated love,

At that moment, I will pompously say that love is nothing
but deceit,

But I wish to hear you say that love is everything,

To conclude, I crave to hear you scream saying that like a
broken pot, a broken heart cannot be mended.

9. EMERALD RESHMA REDDITHOTA

She is Emerald Reshma Reddithota. She completed her graduation in English and Political Science from Hislop College, Nagpur. She loves writing, content creation, travelling, and learning new skills.

UNVOICED HEART

We see people,

Moving on in their lives!

From betrayals and heartbreaks!

But it is not as easy as it seems!

It's not easy to hide your

Emotions, Feelings and Pain!

It's not easy to show a smile

Behind bursting tears!

It's not easy to forget and forgive

People who betrayed us or broke our hearts!

Ifs not easy to let go off

Those people and their beautiful memories with them !

It's not easy to focus and concentrate

On work and other daily activities with that pain !

Their pains often remain unvoiced

With broken hearts !

10. SHUBHANJALI NISHAD

ये नाम शुभांजली निषाद है इनका जन्म 21 दिसंबर को उत्तर प्रदेश के जिले कानपुर में हुआ था । वा इन्होंने अपनी शिक्षा सीजेएसएम यूनिवर्सिटी से पूर्ण की है इनको लिखने का काफी शौक वा इनकी रुचि हिंदी काव्य लेखन में भी है अथवा यह इस पुस्तक "रामनवमी" की संकलन कर्ता भी है । वह 500+ से अधिक संकलनों में सह-लेखक के तौर पर भाग ले चुकी हैं और उन्होंने दो संकलन भी

किये हैं इनकी पहली संकलन पुस्तक का नाम "किसान" और दूसरे संकलन का नाम "फीलिंग्स ऑफ हार्ट" था । इन्हें लिखने के साथ ही पुस्तके पढ़ने वा नई जगहों पर घूमना भी अधिक पसंद करती हैं ।

वह सभी प्रकार की कविताएं लिखने में रुचि रखती है । और उन्हें कल्पनाओं में भ्रमण करना पसंद है उन्हीं कल्पना पर मदद के माध्यम से ये अपने विचारों को कोरे पन्नों में अपनी रचनाओं को खूबसूरती से लिखने कि हुनर रखतीं हैं और इन्होंने अपनी कविता लेखन की माध्यम से कयी रोज़ाना काव्य प्रतियोगिता में भाग लिया है एवं ये कयी प्रतियोगिता में विजय भी हुई है ।

संपर्क करने हेतू : Gmail I'D : nishadrock96@gmail.com

Insta I'd kanha_ki_laado

टाईटल- एक नया दर्द

हर रोज एक नया दर्द दिल

पे दस्तक दे जाता है मेरे

कैसे बंया करूं मैं अपनी

खामोशी एक खामोशी भी

लाखों अश्कों की छाप छोड़

जाती है मेरे दिल पे किसे मैं

कहूं यहां पे अपना कोई अपना

होकर भी पल भर में पराया कर

जाता है मुझे हर रोज उसके ये

नफरत भरे पैगाम कोई है जो

बेतहाशा अंजाने में भी इस दिल

को चोट पहुंचा जाता है दिल से ।।

11. ANVESHITHA

Anveshitha is a mother of 2 kids and a perfect homemaker. She loves to cook in her free time. She found her passion for writing recently and participated in more than 5 anthologies. She is an author in web reading apps like "Kongfubooks" and "Libri". She wants to explore her writing further. Words have the power of everything. It can break you, heal you, make you fall in love with yourself and it also can make you hate yourself.

NOTHING LEFT

I have nothing to gain,

Nothing to lose,

Nothing to achieve,

Nothing to dream of.

I have nothing left to get hurt,

Nothing to bleed,

Nothing to heal.

I have nothing left to say as mine,

To say I can,

To say I do

To say I didn't.

I have nothing left to be save,

Nothing to treasure,

Nothing to hide.

I have nothing left to cry,

Nothing to smile,

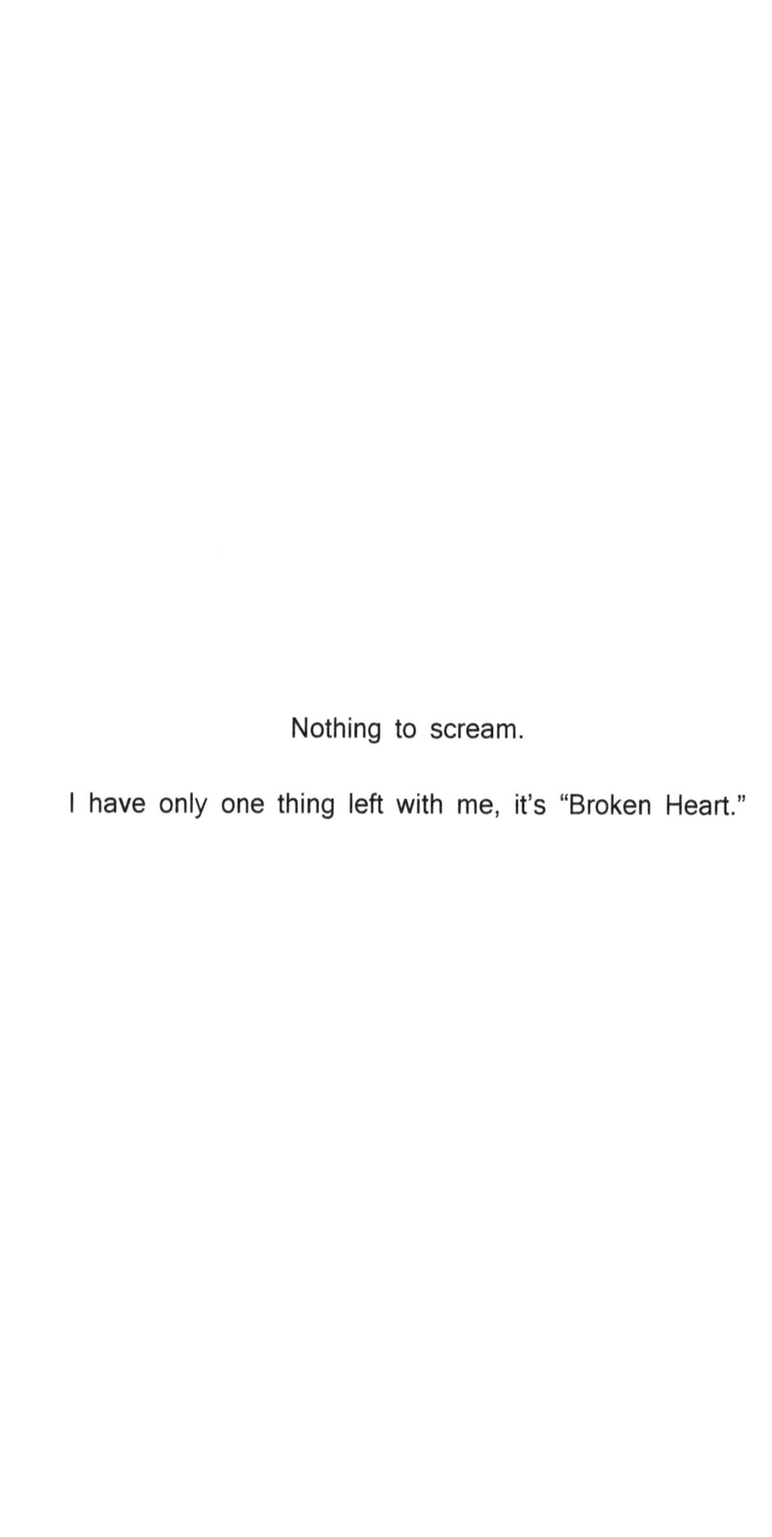

Nothing to scream.

I have only one thing left with me, it's "Broken Heart."

12. NEELAKSH

Neelaksh hails from Lucknow, Uttar Pradesh. He has completed his B.com from Jai Narayan pg college and is pursuing Chartered Accountant. He usually writes as a part of his hobby.

WHY YOU BROKE MY HEART

No one knows how lonely I am

Without you in this world

O my love.....why ....

Do you break my heart....

And left me alone...

Why you Break this beautiful bond...

Of our ..

Don't you remember those beautiful moments....

Which we spent together....

Those dancing in the rain...

Hot coffee date...

That gifts we gave each other...

Why you left me...

O you please come back... My love....

13. MANIK GUPTA

Manik Gupta. He is 23 years old. He is from Shamli(UP) and currently working in Gurgaon. He has already worked as a co-author in more than 30 anthologies and looking forward to more opportunities.

WITHOUT YOU

My heart stops beating,

My mind stops dreaming,

Feels like having someone,

Who can change my fortunes,

You are the only hope I live with,

My only trust,

Hope it remains always,

Hope you always remain you,

Hope my trust pay off on you,

Life would be nothing without you,

Every problem has a solution,

And my solution is just you,

May God shower his blessings on we both,

And never let that time come,

When I am there,

But without you.

14. RANBIR BHAKAT

Author by heart and passion. Writing since He was 16. Ranbir Bhakat is pursuing an integrated undergraduate course in Commerce from Calcutta University, Kolkata. He was born and brought up in Kolkata, West Bengal. His writeups touches reality and reaches everyone's heart. After publishing his own book he wants to explore more. He wants to grasp and grow in his writing journey. His published book is 'Emotions we could never

let out' available in Amazon. His poems can please your broken heart and also please your emotions. Wrote about 30+ Anthologies & 2 Solo Book in preparation.
Gmail: ranbirbhakat5456@gmail.com
Insta Id: @_writing__tales_

INNER ME

I lie awake tonight,

Wishing of things I can change.

I try to convince myself,

But it's all so strange.

Is it me,

Or is it you?

Do I try,

Or are we through?

So long we've shared

Just to walk away.

But so much hurt

To want to stay.

Why do we do this,

Try to hurt the other more,

Only to watch one

Walk right out the door?

15. SHIREESHA M V

Miss Shireesha M V from Karnataka fond of writing Kannada and English poetry.
Pioneers for her motivation as writer was her Hindi teacher Mr. Athikulla and her beloved sisters.
Instagram id: our_blur_image

EMPOWERING IGNORANCE

Served you with serenity

Feeded you amicably

Poured aesthetic emotions

But you gifted matchstick

To our harmony

Greeting flowers as needles

In a breath sentenced

Black to my galaxy of shine!

Yet a ray of hope

To empower my ignorance

In a balcony of brightness.

16. BISHAKHA KUMARI SAXENA

बिशाखा कुमारी सक्सेना जी नोएडा की निवासी हैं और पटना से इन्होनें अपनी सारी शिक्षा पूरी की है। ये समाजशास्त्र में स्नातकोत्तर की उपाधि प्राप्त की हुई है । इनकी रूचि कुकिंग, कविता लेखन, पेंटिंग में है । घर की जिम्मेदारी के कारण नौकरी को छोड़ दिया था । तो पूरी तरह से अपनी रूचि की तरफ ध्यान देना शुरू किया। इन्होनें कुकिंग के प्रतियोगिता में अनेक मैडल, ट्रॉफी, प्रमाण पत्र हासील कर रखा है। इनकी कुकिंग में किताब भी छप चुकी है ।

लेखनी में भी मैगज़ीन और 40 किताबों में इनकी रचनाये छप चुकी है। ये अच्छे विचारो को अपने लेखनी के माध्यम से लोगों तक पंहुचाना चाहती है ।

पहली बार जब दिल टूटा

हाथों की मेहंदी अभी सजी थी,

पैरों की मेहंदी कितनी रँगीली थी,

पलक झपकने से पहले ही दिल उसका टूट गया।

विदा किया था आंधी रात , जब उलझें भी थे

जज़्बात उसके पहले ख़ामोशी से,

ख्वाबों का मंजर भी रूठ गया था।

बॉर्डर पर लड़ाई की खबर पर,

जिंदगी की लहर पर,

संग जीने मरने की रीत जुदा कर हाथ छोड़ साथ छूट गया था।

अब तन्हाईयों का आवरण, खुशियों का अर्थ,

राहो से लिपटकर तो,

आसमानों में उड़कर लूट गया था

हाथों की मेहंदी अभी सजी थी

, पैरों की मेहंदी कितनी रँगीली थी

, पलक झपकने से पहले ही दिल उसका टूट गया।

विदा किया था आंधी रात, जब उलझें भी थे

जज़्बात उसके पहले ख़ामोशी से,

ख्वाबों का मंजर भी रूठ गया था।

बॉर्डर पर लड़ाई की खबर पर,

जिंदगी की लहर पर,

संग जीने मरने की रीत जुदा कर हाथ छोड़ साथ छूट गया था।

अब तन्हाईयों का आवरण, खुशियों का अर्थ,

राहो से लिपटकर तो,

आसमानों में उड़कर लूट गया था।

हाथों की मेहंदी अभी सजी थी,

पैरों की मेहंदी कितनी रँगीली थी ,

पलक झपकने से पहले ही दिल उसका टूट गया।

विदा किया था आंधी रात, जब उलझें भी थे

जज़्बात उसके पहले ख़ामोशी से,

ख्वाबों का मंजर भी रूठ गया था।

बॉर्डर पर लड़ाई की खबर पर,

जिंदगी की लहर पर,

संग जीने मरने की रीत जुदा कर हाथ छोड़ साथ छूट गया था।

अब तन्हाईयों का आवरण, खुशियों का अर्थ,

राहो से लिपटकर तो,

आसमानों में उड़कर लूट गया था।

हाथों की मेहंदी अभी सजी थी

, पैरों की मेहंदी कितनी रँगीली थी

, पलक झपकने से पहले ही दिल उसका टूट गया।

विदा किया था आंधी रात, जब उलझें भी थे

जज़्बात उसके पहले ख़ामोशी से,

ख्वाबों का मंजर भी रूठ गया था।

बॉर्डर पर लड़ाई की खबर पर,

जिंदगी की लहर पर,

संग जीने मरने की रीत जुदा कर हाथ छोड़ साथ छूट गया था।

अब तन्हाईयों का आवरण, खुशियों का अर्थ,

राहो से लिपटकर तो,

आसमानों में उड़कर लूट गया था।

हाथों की मेहंदी अभी सजी थी

, पैरों की मेहंदी कितनी रँगीली थी

, पलक झपकने से पहले ही दिल उसका टूट गया।

विदा किया था आंधी रात, जब उलझें भी थे

जज़्बात उसके पहले ख़ामोशी से,

ख्वाबों का मंजर भी रूठ गया था।

बॉर्डर पर लड़ाई की खबर पर,

जिंदगी की लहर पर,

संग जीने मरने की रीत जुदा कर हाथ छोड़ साथ छूट गया था।

अब तन्हाईयों का आवरण, खुशियों का अर्थ,

राहो से लिपटकर तो,

आसमानों में उड़कर लूट गया था।

17. RAGHAVI RAGHU

Raghavi Raghu is 19 years old, she passed Class 12 from Sunshine senior secondary school, Chennai and is now doing her Bachelor's degree in advanced zoology and biotechnology at JBAS College for Women. Apart from writing she also pursues sketching, reading books and debating as interests. A huge bibliophile herself and has a vivid love for new experiences in life. She is just like the girl next door living in a bustling city with huge dreams and hopes that are just as sophisticated as her. Writing has not just been her passion but also her driving force to success and expresses thoughts and emotions in a new way that the world is starting to notice and leads a life that is both challenging and successful and experiencing a wide contrast while balancing two widely different mind sets of the society.

TIME

I thought I lost you,

But you helped

Me find myself from

The time wrap I was Stuck in.

I thought I hurt you,

But you helped me

Heal from the wounds of my past.

I thought I loved you more,

But you loved

Me more than the

Time could keep track Off.

I thought you wouldn't stay,

But you held me in

Me in your arms and

Said "until the time

Stops I won't leave You."

I thought you were the one,

No buts and time

Made me realize it.

18. SALMA KHAN

Salma khan is from . Her graduated from Devi Ahilya Vishwavidyalaya indore. Her hobbies are reading-writing , drowning, singing. Keep naturals & creative thoughts. She's started writing in month of October 2021. Her thoughts are part of co-author in many anthologies

MERI TRUE LOVE STORY

Aaj mai aapse apni mohobbat ki kahani share karne ja rahi hu ….meri true love story .

Dosto suna hai Sachi mohobbat ankho se shuru hokar Rooh tak pahuchti hai …….

Hamari mohobbat bhi same aisy hi thi ….

Ek din sham ko main gahr ke bahar baithi thi aur tabhi rashte se uska gujarna hua……

Naa jane kya kashish thi usme main bas

Uski taraf khichti hi chali gai ….

Ek din meri friend uske boy friend se milne gai wo mujhe bhi sath le kar gai thi ….

Jab uska bf aaya tab uske sath uska ek friend bhi tha ……aur dosto main uske dost ko bas dekhte hl reh gai kyoki uska dost wo hi ladka tha jise mene apni gali mein dekha tha …..ye ittefaq tha ya khuda koi ishara tha ….mere liye mujhe usse milane ka ….

Thode din baad usne mujhe prapose Kiya …

Mene bhi Han kar di kyoki mein use phli najar se hi chahne lagi thi .. .hamare pyar ki kahani aage badi …hum dono milne lage

Bahut saari baatein hui ….kai kasme vaade

Kiye ham dono ne ….lekin shadi ke liye ham dono ka ek hi disision tha , ki ham dono hamari family ki marji se hi shadi karenge …

Aur agar kisi ek ki bhi family hamare rishte ke liye , shadi ke liye mana karegi to ham dono shadi nahi karenge….fir ek din uski masi ki ladki ka rishta uske liye aaya …uski family ne uski masi ko shadi ke rishte ke liye haa kar di …usne manane ki bahut koshish ki apni family ko hamare rishte ke liye , lekin wo log unki masi ko haa kar chuke the ….

Dosto bhag kar hum dono shadi nahi karna chahte the …isliye uski shadi uski masi ki ladki ke sath ho gai ….usne mera sath majburi mein chhoda tha wo bewafa nahi

Tha aur uske disision par mujhe aaj bhi naaj hai …usne jo kuchh bhi kiya apni family ki ijjat aur khushi ke liye kiya …last mulakat par hum dono bahut roye the , ek dusre ko hamne last time gift bhi diya the ..jo Aaj bhi mere pass hai …aaj bhi mai use bahut Miss karti hu …. Shayad use bhi kabhi meri yaad aati hogi ab hamara koi contact nahi hai…..

I hope , dosto apko meri true love story pasand aai hogi …

19. AABID SUBZAR

Young "Aabid Subzar" a 16 years old resident of Odura Kulgam of South Kashmir is a Student of Class 12th. Author has been writing since Childhood and a dream of becoming a Successful poet dances in his auricles. He been has been writing quotes,Short stories,poems from a very long. Aabid Subzar is a young boy who wants to make a big difference in the Society.He is a humble soul from a rustic background. He has been bestowed with this gift of penning poetry via literacy gifted to him by her motherland He aspires to achieve great things and wants to serve the nation. The real scope of his poetry flows from each line of his poems.So far Author has co-authored 25+ books.

Author can be mailed at : aabidsubzar@gmail.com

THE UNVOICED

The Unvoiced

My heart has enough to say to the world

But the cruel nature of world took control

It had a long tale to describe

Yet it has tongue but no voice

The worldly baseless faiths enriched it

With a long depresssing and worrying behaviour

Had to tell the world about my soulmate

No one had ears who could lend to it

Everyone made a fun of it

None paid heed to its words

Its auricles yet flow the blood through it

None paid attention to the oozing blood

Yet this pumping muscle beats continue

In a hope to see the light in the pure dark.

20. KAMINI PRADHAN

कामिनी प्रधान ,पिता - मंगल प्रसाद प्रधान , माता -तपोवंती प्रधान , जो ग्राम पंचायत -आमगांव ,शाखा - तमनार, जिला रायगढ़ छत्तीसगढ़ से रहने वाली है, जो अभी एम.एस.सी रसायन शास्त्र में अध्ययनरत है, जो पढ़ने , लिखने के साथ ही संगीत में रुचि रखती हैं ।

कहते कुछ नहीं

कहते कुछ नही

टूटा हुआ साज हु मै , किसी के दिल की आवाज हूँ मैं ,

अपनी बात सुनानी है टूटा हुआ एक राज हूँ मैं,

दिन बहुत हो गया याद आती है उसकी परछाई बस गई ,

यादों में मेरे साथ एक किताब खाली पड़ी रही है ,

बस जीवन में बहार आने की कमी है ,

खुली किताबो में रंग बिखेरना बाकी है ,

सफेद पन्ने में यादों का तशरीफ जारी है ,

लिखने को काबिल है मगर सुनने वाले का पता नही ,

सर झुका लेते है अपनी , जिंदगी बनाकर बसा लेते है ,

जानने ताला अब भी बात समझता होगा क्या ,

आसू देखकर भी जो मुड़कर पीछे पलटा ही नही ,

वो राज छुपा रहा है , सुनना है उसकी बातो को सुनना ,

वो आँखों को और गीली करता जा रहा ,

पता नही क्यों अपनी हर बात छुपाता है ,

कह देता समझ जाते हम पल दो पल की जिंदगी जी लेते हम ,

सवाल हम बहुत मगर बात हमारी उनसे होती नहीं ।।

21. NAYAN DATEY

इनका नाम नयन दाते है ये एक छात्र हैं । जो की महाराष्ट्र के जिले पूणें में रहते हैं । आंखों अपने विचार शब्दों में प्रकट करने का शौख है ये एक लेखक हैं ।

Andaaz E ISHQ

Andaaz e ishq unka

Humko sab keh gaya

Ye khuda ka banda

Aaj bhi akela reh gaya

Mushkil se hasil hui thi

Humko unki mohobbat

Juda unse hote hi

Mere dil ka dariya beh gaya

Mar chuka hai dil Mara

Jism me saansein baaki hai

Ab unki talaash nahi hume

Unki yaadein kaafi hai...

22. SANAT KUMAR MISHRA

He is Sanat kumar Mishra a boy, studying in Class-12. He is a writer and a pretty well artist. He was born and brought up In cuttack, odIsha. He feels immensely pleasured to write poems about emotions & upheavals in life. He entered the arena of literature not long before 4 years when he wrote his first poem in English.

HIS HEART CRIPPLED

HIS HEART CRIPPLED

There exists a statue who was once a man;

The truth of life left him alive but with no soul.

Once cheerful & glowing in all deadly span,

Jeered at every disastrous strife & get goal.

Once marching in a dark forest with lust;

Hurdling the cheerful path to success-

Witnessed a hardship that ultimately crushed.

He drenches himself under the pensive rainy tears-

Of mourning moist clouds hovering over mind.

Dissented from the blooming road with no sheer;

Ultimately brought about a slave of all winds-

That jams the human soul due to the arduous life.

The grievances of the event dwelled over his agile:

Cemented the immense courage of the man with strife,

And! Taken aback with the monotonous tread-

At last his heart crippled and he became a-

Heartless statue due to the affliction of hard life..

But still received a blissful shower of sunshine

Giving him a new streak of hope to march ahead

Along the glorious victory line!

(This poem describes about a man who was not able to fulfill his dreams once in his lifetime. Even he lost as all his near ones due to a great mishap once in a life. This made him depressed,grasped up his courage, lost his determination and was grieved. And his heart was crippled. But later he witnessed a shower of hope from someone that restored his zeal & positive outlook towards life.)

23. SWATHI R

she is a biotechnology student and she is constant learner . she wanna be a author.

MY EYES AREN'T GONNA SHINE ANYMORE

I can't have the hope to live,

I don't have a reason to breath,

I have lost the faith in life,

I don't have the courage to smile,

I can't forget anything either,

O not broken, it's just my heart which is broken.

24. AMRUTHA C

A physics graduate that loves to write the feelings that are treasured under the face mask. Lives in Chennai and lives to paint the picture in words. A person who can do both extremes, Logics, and creativity. Love, joy, sadness, happiness, excitement, grief, anger, fear, anticipation, and many more emotions make us feel humane. Might not have experienced all of this in the personal life but experienced these through writing.

OH,HEART,YOU WERE THE ONE

Oh, heart, you were the one

Who started to get excited at the sight of him.

Now, you are the one who gets broken

Whenever he is mentioned.

Your job is only to pump blood,

But you have taken upon over the world

To fall in love with someone who

Doesn't know how to reciprocate,

How to appreciate and handle you.

It ain't really your fault, you are just

Veined like that, turning all of this into vain.

You aren't to be blamed, because

It is what it is.

25. RITU

Hello friends She is Ritu from delhi 10th class student and she has been co-author in many anthologies.

SAMJHA LIJIYE

Baato ki gehraayia itni thi ki,

Usme girna manzoor ni tha...

Baato Mai sachaai itni ki

, Unhe manna mumkin nhi tha.

.. Zindagi bhi kitni ajeeb hoti hai,

Aaj koi hai kal nhi...

Lekin jb wo apse dur chale jaaye,

To khudko samjha lijiye...

Unke sath rehna mukkadar mai nhi tha...

Apki khaamoshi hi apki kamzori hai,

Or unki muskurat apki taqat...

Agr unke dur chale jaane mai unki khusi hai to,

Khamosh rehne mai koi harz nhi...

Jhoot hi saii.. Ek baar keh dete...

Humse dur rehna apke liye munasib nhi tha...

Zindagi mai kamiyabi to de di hai...

Bas ek dafa apse sunna chahtii hu..

Jo maine mehsoos kiya wo pyar nhi tha...

26. ISHITA

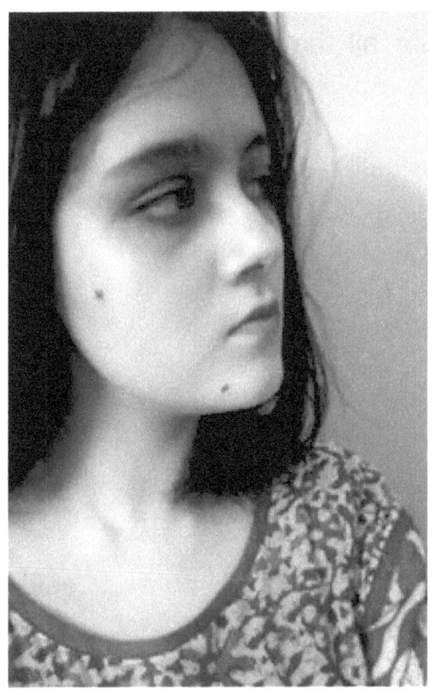

Born in January 2003 in kolkata , West Bengal studied till class 12 at St. Pauls boarding and day school, Kolkata.Currently pursuing BBA(Hospital Management) in NSHM Knowledge Campus, Kolkata . She has been writing poems ever since she was in class 6.Some of her works has also have been published in some local newspapers like The Telegraph(TTIS) and school magazines.Her poems have been featured in the book THE LAST FLOWER OF SPRING by Poem Pajama publications under Delhi Poerty Slam. "WHISPER OF HEARTS" by Bookfever publications and " MIRAKEE " by TGIWC.She also wants to write more in future and inspire all the sections of the society.

A BETTER PLACE

Through the half opened door

The vermillion liquid flowed

And covered the floor

Towards the edge lay her lifeless hand

Nothing was left to be said

Nothing was there to understand

Tears mixed with blood

What a pleasant sight

Too bad, she gave one of her own

Bones to others in their fights

Burnt her ownself to give others light

Gave her own food to the needy

And fed on poison at night

Yet endured the violence within her silence

Hope she is now in a better place

With a smile on her face.

27. SAPANA S BAIN

What more you expect if someone loves you not over his death but he wants to live with you, grow old with you, cuddle and cherish all moments with you, keep memories to make candid, fight with you love you, kiss you, even shed your tears, etch your name on his soul forever, even not beside him he feels you. Like a forbidden fruit he craves for you. And you yourself as a mist falls on him and smile on the corner of his lips and disappear just like a figment in imagination. Playing with words & aligning them to provoke the dead feelings at a snap of finger is one of the best way of a writer to get reborn in hearts of their fans. Being born & brought in the heart of India Madhya Pradesh she pursued her dreams. Not only she excelled in academics but as a singer, dancer, Sketch artist she Couldn't refrain herself from bursting out her feelings, her emotions as writing. She's a published writer, co-author of numbers of anthologies she's down to earth type personality. Let's get spelled by the magic created by her in her write ups in her own world.

LONE TEARS

Lone tears

It was you distanced & so afar

I couldn't find with blink of my sight as ajar

It was me loitering here & there just to search you

& at last I got disappeared in dark hue

It was a promise we will meet at dawn

When the crimson tint hit the horizon

Why this waves ,this air got stuck somewhere

My heart didn't want to understand that why it happened
unfair

This endurance got iced in eyes

& slumber became mirage which always defies

No one likes me as you did

No one loves me as you did

With hopeless heart in my bony cage

I became habitual of this endurance & rage

That fake smile of people which always kept enticing

& that erroneous calm world always kept spicing

Oh! My love we dreamed of a life together to make it
candid

But it got swiped and wiped from our existence by bandit

Only the scars got remained as pathetic pain

No one likes me as you did

No one loves me as you did....

www.ingramcontent.com/pod-product-compliance
Lightning Source LLC
Chambersburg PA
CBHW022023150726

47990CB00002B/781